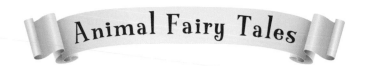

The Emperor Penguin's New Clothes

written by Charlotte Guillain ☆ illustrated by Dawn Beacon

Raintree

Chicago, Illinois

To contact Capstone Global Library please call 800-747-4992, or visit our web site
www.capstonepub.com

Edited by Daniel Nunn, Rebecca Rissman, and Catherine Veitch
Designed by Joanna Hinton-Malivoire
Original illustrations © Capstone Global Library, Ltd, 2014
Illustrated by Dawn Beacon
Production by Victoria Fitzgerald
Originated by Capstone Global Library, Ltd
Printed and bound in China

17 16 15 14 13
10 9 8 7 6 5 4 3 2 1

Library of Congress Cataloging-in-Publication Data
Guillain, Charlotte.
  The emperor penguin's new clothes / Charlotte Guillain.
    pages cm—(Animal fairy tales)
ISBN 978-1-4109-6114-3 (hb)—ISBN 978-1-4109-6121-1 (pb) [1. Fairy tales.] I. Andersen,
H. C. (Hans Christian), 1805-1875. Kejserens nye kl?der. English. II. Title.
PZ8.G947Em 2014
[E]--dc23   2013011476

Characters

Emperor Penguin

Penguin Servant

Killer Whale

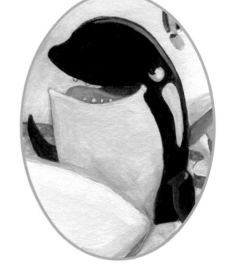

Subjects

There was once a snowy land that was ruled by Emperor Penguin.

Every morning he would stand on a hill to look down at all the other penguins and feel very important.

One day Emperor Penguin was
watching all the other penguins on
the ice when Killer Whale popped up
out of the sea and looked at him.

"You look very important," said Killer Whale.

"Oh, I am," said Emperor Penguin snootily. "I am the emperor of all penguins. I am much more special than all these other penguins."

Killer Whale looked around and sighed.
"It's a shame. You look just the same
as all these other penguins," he said.

"Someone as important as you
should surely look different from
everyone else."

Emperor Penguin was shocked. "You're right!" he said. "Everyone should see that I am more special than other penguins."

"I will help you," said Killer Whale. "Bring me a thousand fish, and I will make you look special."

So Emperor Penguin made his servants
catch one thousand fish and take them
to Killer Whale. Then Killer Whale
gobbled up the fish, and he looked at
the emperor.

"This is what you need
to do," he whispered in
Emperor Penguin's ear.

The next morning, all the penguins woke
up and went about their business. As usual,
Emperor Penguin took his place standing
on the hill looking down on everyone.

"Um, your majesty," said a nervous servant, "You've forgotten to put on your clothes!"

17

"Ha!" scoffed Emperor Penguin.
"You fool! I'm wearing a special suit
that Killer Whale gave me. He told
me that it would be invisible to foolish,
ordinary penguins."

Emperor Penguin paraded across
the ice, proudly declaring, "See how
important I am? My new suit is so
special that only I can see it!"
The other penguins watched him
pass by as he started to shiver.

A small penguin chick shouted,
"Look at that silly penguin! He's
forgotten to put on his clothes!"

All the other penguins laughed, and
Emperor Penguin realized how foolish
he had been. From that day on, he wore
warm clothes like the other penguins. And
he never listened to Killer Whale again!

The End

Where does this story come from?

You've probably already heard the story that *The Emperor Penguin's New Clothes* is based on—*The Emperor's New Clothes*. There are many different versions of this story. When people tell a story, they often make little changes to make it their own. How would you change this story?

The history of the story

The Emperor's New Clothes was written by Hans Christian Andersen. Andersen was born in 1805 and lived in Denmark. He wrote many poems and stories, including many fairy tales. Andersen's fairy stories became famous around the world.

In the original story, a foolish, vain emperor is tricked by two weavers. They sell him a suit of fine clothes that they claim is only visible to the most important and intelligent people. The emperor can't see anything, but he doesn't want to be thought of as unimportant or stupid. He claims that he loves the suit and allows the weavers to "dress" him in it. When he goes out wearing nothing, everyone is too scared to say anything, even though he is naked. Finally, a small child says what everyone is thinking, and the emperor is shown to be a fool.